Copyright Page

Conscientious Casino Table Gambler: A Dummy Guidebook
Author: Sunny Wang, Ph.D.
Edition: First Edition
Publication Date: June 2024

Copyright © 2024 by Dr. Sunny Wang. All rights reserved.
No part of this book may be reproduced, distributed, or transmitted in any form or by any means, including photocopying, recording, or other electronic or mechanical methods, without the prior written permission of the publisher, except in the case of brief quotations embodied in critical reviews and certain other non-commercial uses permitted by copyright law. For permission requests, write to the book marketplace provider.

Disclaimer:
The information provided in this book is for educational and informational purposes only. The author and publisher are not responsible for any losses or damages that may occur as a result of applying the information provided in this book. Gambling involves risk, and readers should gamble responsibly and within their financial means.

Trademarks:
All trademarks, product names, and company names or logos cited herein are the property of their respective owners. The inclusion of any trademarks does not imply endorsement or affiliation with the author or publisher.

This book is dedicated to fellow gamblers.

Reap from my experience.

Dr. Sunny Wang

Table of Contents

Introduction **5**
Personal Experience 5
The Purpose of This Guide 5
Understanding the Odds 6
Chapter Highlights 6
Why Read This Guide 7

Chapter 1: The Reality of Casino Gambling **8**
House Edge and Its Impact 8
Short-Term vs. Long-Term Outcomes 9
Probability and Randomness 11
The Psychology of Gambling 12

Chapter 2: The Mechanics of Baccarat **14**
Game Table Layout 14
Variations of Baccarat 14
Game Rules 15
Third Card Drawing Rules 16
House Edge and Commission 17
Basic Betting Strategy 18

Chapter 3: Betting Systems and Their Flaws **19**
The Labouchere Betting System 19
The Martingale Betting System 20
The Paroli Betting System 21
The Fibonacci Betting System 22
Why Betting Systems Fail 22
What Does "Never Chase Losses" Mean? 23

Chapter 4: Money Management Myths **25**
Setting Win Goals and Loss Limits 25
The Myth of "Hot" and "Cold" Streaks 25
The Falsehood of Money Management Systems 26
The Importance of Proper Bankroll Management 26

Chapter 5: The Illusion of Trends **28**
Understanding Independence of Events 28
The Gambler's Fallacy 28
The Illusion of Control 29

The Role of Trend Betting	29
Statistical Analysis and Randomness	29
Chapter 6: Effective Strategies for Conscientious Gambling	**31**
Even Bet	31
Flat Betting	31
Set Limits	32
Avoid Chasing Losses	32
Treat Gambling as Entertainment	33
Importance of Research and Knowledge	33
Maintain a Balanced Lifestyle	34
Recognizing and Addressing Problem Gambling	34
Conclusion	**36**
Recap of Key Points	36
Final Thoughts	37
Appendices	**38**
Glossary of Gambling Terms	38
Additional Resources	39

Introduction

Welcome to "Conscientious Casino Table Gambler: A Dummy Guidebook." This book is designed to help low- to middle-income or risk-averse gamblers navigate the complex world of casino table games. Drawing from my personal experiences of significant financial losses and hard-learned lessons, this guide aims to equip you with the knowledge and strategies needed to gamble responsibly and enjoy the experience without falling into the common pitfalls that many gamblers face.

Personal Experience

Over the span of a year, I found myself repeatedly drawn to the baccarat table, hoping to turn the odds in my favor. Using the Labouchere Betting System, a negative progression system where you increase your stake after every consecutive loss, I aimed to recover my losses and achieve significant wins. However, the reality was far from my expectations. Despite my efforts and the use of various strategies, I ended up losing a substantial five-figure sum. Each loss was a blow not just to my bankroll but also to my morale, leading to immense stress and anxiety.

This guide is born out of that difficult journey. My goal is to share these experiences not to discourage you from gambling, but to provide you with a realistic understanding of the risks involved and the strategies that can help mitigate those risks. Gambling can be thrilling, but it is essential to approach it with caution, knowledge, and a clear strategy.

The Purpose of This Guide

This guide aims to:

- **Educate:** Provide a thorough understanding of the realities of casino gambling.
- **Inform:** Offer insights into the structure and rules of various casino table games.
- **Debunk:** Explain why common betting systems and strategies often fail.
- **Advise:** Offer practical advice on how to gamble responsibly.
- **Encourage:** Promote a mindset that views gambling as a form of entertainment rather than a way to make money.

By understanding the mechanics of casino games and recognizing the fallacies in popular betting systems, you can approach gambling with a more informed and cautious mindset. The ultimate goal is to foster a community of gamblers who can enjoy the experience responsibly and avoid significant financial losses.

Understanding the Odds

One of the most critical lessons I've learned is that all commercially run gambling games are designed to ensure the casino's advantage. Over hundreds or thousands of bets, the house edge will always result in losses for the player. This guide will delve into the mathematics behind this reality, providing statistical tables that illustrate both short-term and long-term betting outcomes.

For instance, in baccarat, the house edge on a "Banker" bet is around 1.06% and for a "Player" bet, it's about 1.24%. While these percentages might seem small, over time they ensure that the casino will always win more than it loses. In roulette, the addition of a single zero or double zero significantly increases the house edge, making it impossible for players to maintain long-term winnings.

Chapter Highlights

Chapter 1: The Reality of Casino Gambling

Casino gambling is inherently risky. Every game in the casino, whether it's baccarat, roulette, blackjack, or sic bo, is designed to give the house an edge over the players. This chapter explores the fundamental principles of casino gambling and the statistical inevitability of losses over time.

Chapter 2: The Mechanics of Baccarat

Baccarat is one of the most popular casino games, and understanding its mechanics is crucial for any conscientious gambler. This chapter provides a detailed look at the rules and variations of baccarat.

Chapter 3: Betting Systems and Their Flaws

Many gamblers turn to betting systems in an attempt to overcome the house edge. This chapter examines popular betting systems and explains why they ultimately fail.

Chapter 4: Money Management Myths

Just as betting systems are flawed, so too are many money management strategies. This chapter debunks common money management myths and emphasizes the importance of responsible gambling.

Chapter 5: The Illusion of Trends

Casinos often display past play results to create the illusion of trends, suggesting that future outcomes can be predicted based on previous ones. This chapter explains why this is a fallacy and how each game round is independent of the previous ones.

Chapter 6: Effective Strategies for Conscientious Gambling

To gamble responsibly and minimize losses, consider the following strategies. These approaches focus on making informed decisions, managing your bankroll effectively, and maintaining discipline throughout your gambling sessions. Recognizing signs of problem gambling and treating gambling as entertainment are crucial for responsible gambling. This chapter provides tips for staying disciplined and enjoying gambling responsibly.

Why Read This Guide

This guide is designed to help you walk into any casino, choose your preferred table game, and play as a conscientious gambler. By understanding the rules, odds, and the fallacies of betting systems, you can make informed decisions and enjoy gambling as a form of entertainment rather than a money-making venture. Remember, the key to responsible gambling is knowledge, discipline, and the ability to walk away when necessary.

Chapter 1: The Reality of Casino Gambling

Casino gambling is inherently risky. Every game in the casino, whether it's baccarat, roulette, blackjack, or sic bo, is designed to give the house an edge over the players. This chapter explores the fundamental principles of casino gambling and the statistical inevitability of losses over time.

House Edge and Its Impact

The house edge is the mathematical advantage that the casino has over the players. It ensures that the casino will make a profit in the long run. Understanding this concept is crucial for any gambler. Here's how the house edge works in different games:

- **Roulette:**
  - In European roulette, the house edge is 2.70% with only a single zero "0".
    - This is calculated as the ratio of the house's expected loss to the player's original bet.
    - The house edge can be derived from the fact that there is one "0" slot in addition to the 36 numbered slots.
    - The probability of a player who bets on "Red" or "Black" shall lose when the roulette ball lands on "0" is

    $$\frac{1}{37} = 0.027 \; or \; 2.70\%.$$

  - In American roulette, the house edge is 5.26% due to the inclusion of a single zero "0" and a double zero "00".
- **Baccarat:**
  - The house edge on the "Banker" bet is approximately 1.06%.
  - The house edge on the "Player" bet is about 1.24%.
  - Although these percentages seem small, over thousands of hands, they add up to significant losses for the player.
- **Blackjack:**
  - The house edge can vary depending on the rules of the table and the player's skill. On average, it is around 0.50% for skilled players.
- **Sic Bo:**
  - The house edge varies greatly depending on the type of bet, ranging from 2.78% to as high as 30%.

The house edge ensures that over time, the casino will always win more money than it pays out. This is a fundamental truth that all gamblers must accept.

Below is a table comparing the house edge of various popular casino games. Higher house edge lowers the players chance of winning.

Casino Game	House Edge
Blackjack	0.50% - 1% (with optimal strategy)
Roulette (European)	2.70%
Roulette (American)	5.26%
Craps (Pass Line Bet)	1.41%
Baccarat (Banker Bet)	1.06%
Baccarat (Player Bet)	1.24%
Baccarat (Tie Bet)	14.36%
Slots	2% - 15%
Video Poker	0.46% - 5%
Three Card Poker	1.50% - 3.37%
Pai Gow Poker	1.46%
Keno	25% - 29%
Caribbean Stud Poker	5.22%
Let It Ride	3.51%

Table 1. This table provides an overview of the typical house edge percentages for some of the most common casino games. Note that the house edge can vary based on specific game rules and player strategy.

Short-Term vs. Long-Term Outcomes

While it is possible to have short-term winning streaks, the long-term expectation is always in favor of the house. This section will illustrate the difference between short-term variance and long-term certainty through charts and statistical tables.

Example:

- A player might experience a winning streak over 100 hands, but over 1,000 hands, the house edge will inevitably lead to losses.
- Here are the tables displaying a roulette "Red" color plus $1 flat bets. Tables Table 2 and Table 3 illustrate the bet outcomes for every 20 spins, while Table 4 summarizes the bet results in groups of 100 spins. At the end of 1000 spins, there was an overall loss of $42 for a $1 wager amount on "Red".

Spin Number	Bet Outcome
1-20	-2
21-40	-2
41-60	0
61-80	-10
81-100	-2

Total	-16

Table 2. First 100 spins.

Spin Number	Bet Outcome
101-120	8
121-140	-2
141-160	-8
161-180	4
181-200	-8
Total	-6

Table 3. Next 100 spins.

Spin Number	Bet Outcome
1-100	-16
101-200	-6
201-300	-8
301-400	4
401-500	4
501-600	-10
601-700	-6
701-800	4
801-900	8
901-1000	-12
Total	**-42**

Table 4. Full 1000 spins summary.

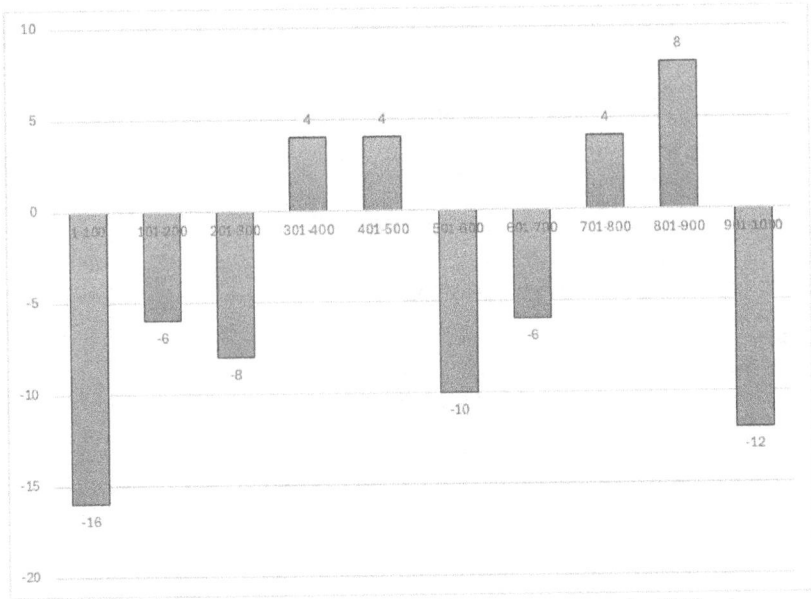

Figure 1. Graphic illustration of Table 4's wager outcomes for 1000 spins.

Probability and Randomness

Understanding probability and randomness is key to understanding why casinos always have the advantage. Each game outcome is independent of previous outcomes, meaning that past results do not influence future results. This concept is crucial for avoiding the gambler's fallacy – the mistaken belief that past events can influence future outcomes.

Example:

- In roulette, each spin is independent of the previous spin. The odds of hitting a "Red", "Black", "Even", "Odd", "Low", or "High" number remain the same regardless of past results.
- For European roulette:
  - There are 18 red slots, 18 black slots, and one "0" green slot out of the 37 total slots.
  - The probability of landing on a red or black slot is calculated as:

    Number of red slots/Total slots =

$$\frac{18}{37} = 0.4865 \text{ or } 48.65\%$$

Number of black slots/Total slots =

$$\frac{18}{37} = 0.4865 \text{ or } 48.65\%$$

- This probability stays the same at the first, second, third, fourth, ..., or tenth spin, as shown in Table 5.

Spin Number	Red (%)	Black (%)	Even (%)	Odd (%)	Low (1-18) (%)	High (19-36) (%)
1	48.65	48.65	48.65	48.65	48.65	48.65
2	48.65	48.65	48.65	48.65	48.65	48.65
3	48.65	48.65	48.65	48.65	48.65	48.65
4	48.65	48.65	48.65	48.65	48.65	48.65
5	48.65	48.65	48.65	48.65	48.65	48.65
6	48.65	48.65	48.65	48.65	48.65	48.65
7	48.65	48.65	48.65	48.65	48.65	48.65
8	48.65	48.65	48.65	48.65	48.65	48.65
9	48.65	48.65	48.65	48.65	48.65	48.65
10	48.65	48.65	48.65	48.65	48.65	48.65

Table 5. The odds remain the same for every spin of the roulette wheel.

The Psychology of Gambling

Casinos leverage psychological principles to encourage continued play. Understanding these principles can help gamblers make more informed decisions and recognize when they are being influenced by the environment.

- **Illusion of Control:** Players often believe they can influence the outcome of a game through skill or strategy, even in games of pure chance.
- **Near Misses:** Games are designed to create near-miss situations, which encourage players to keep playing in the hope of an imminent win.
- **Comp Rewards:** Casinos offer complimentary rewards (comps) to keep players engaged and loyal.

By understanding the reality of casino gambling, players can make more informed decisions and enjoy their time at the casino responsibly. The key is to recognize the inherent risks, understand the house edge, and approach gambling as a form of entertainment rather than a way to make money.

Chapter 2: The Mechanics of Baccarat

Baccarat is one of the most popular casino games, and understanding its mechanics is crucial for any conscientious gambler. This chapter provides a detailed look at the rules and variations of baccarat.

Game Table Layout

An example of a table layout with designated areas for placing "Player", "Banker", "Tie", "Player Pair", and "Banker Pair" bets is shown below.

Figure 2. Sample of a baccarat table layout with 1 to 7 playing positions.

Variations of Baccarat

- **Punto Banco:**
  - **Description:** Punto Banco is the most commonly played version of baccarat in casinos worldwide.
  - **Gameplay:** In Punto Banco, the casino banks the game at all times and commits to playing both hands according to fixed drawing rules. Players can bet on either the player's hand ("Punto"), the banker's hand ("Banco"), or a tie. The game is largely based on chance, with no strategic decision-making for the players once the bets are placed.
  - **Objective:** The objective is to predict which hand will have a total value closest to 9.
- **Chemin de Fer:**

- **Description:** Chemin de Fer is a French variation of baccarat. It translates to "railway" in English and is known for its slower pace compared to Punto Banco.
- **Gameplay:** In Chemin de Fer, players take turns being the banker. The role of the banker rotates counterclockwise around the table. Players have more influence over the game as they can choose whether or not to draw a third card, adding a level of skill and strategy.
- **Objective:** Similar to other versions, the goal is to achieve a hand value closest to 9, but players' decisions can affect the outcome.

- **Baccarat Banque:**
  - **Description:** Baccarat Banque is similar to Chemin de Fer but has some distinct differences. It is also of French origin.
  - **Gameplay:** In Baccarat Banque, the banker position is more permanent compared to Chemin de Fer. The banker role is often auctioned off to the highest bidder, and the banker remains in the position until they decide to retire or run out of funds. This version is typically played with three decks of cards.
  - **Objective:** The aim is to bet on the hand that will have a total value closest to 9, but the permanent banker adds a unique dynamic to the game.

Game Rules

While baccarat has several variations, including Punto Banco, Chemin de Fer, and Baccarat Banque, the core objective remains the same – to bet on the hand closest to nine – the rules and play styles can vary. Here are the basic rules common to most versions:

- **Card Decks:**
  - The game of Baccarat is typically played with four to ten decks of cards, with each deck having 52 cards without joker cards and with backs of the same color and design. For a game that uses eight decks of cards, there would be 416 cards handled in total.
- **Card Values:**

Card	Value
Ace	1
2	2
3	3
4	4
5	5
6	6

7	7
8	8
9	9
10	0
Jack (J)	0
Queen (Q)	0
King (K)	0

- Suits do not matter.
- Aces are worth 1 point.
- 2 through 9 are worth their face value.
- 10s and face cards (Jacks, Queens, Kings) are worth 0 points.
- The values of the cards are added together, and only the last digit of the sum is used. For example, a hand with a 7 and a 9 would have a value of 6 (since 7 + 9 = 16, and the last digit is 6).

- **Gameplay:**
    - Players bet on either the "Player" hand, the "Banker" hand, or a tie.
    - Two cards are dealt to both the Player and Banker hands.
    - If either hand totals 8 or 9 (a "natural"), no further cards are drawn.
    - If neither hand has a natural, the Player hand may draw a third card based on specific rules.
    - The Banker hand then draws a third card based on more complex rules which consider the Player's third card.
- **Objective:**
    - The hand closest to a total of 9 wins.
    - If both hands have the same total, the round results in a tie. The initial wagers on "Player" and "Banker" do not win or lose in this case, but all "Tie wagers" win.

Third Card Drawing Rules

The drawing rules in baccarat can seem complex, but here are some easy-to-understand bullet points to make them effortless to remember:

- **For the Player:**
    - **Total of 0-5**: The Player draws a third card.
    - **Total of 6 or 7**: The Player stands.
    - **Total of 8 or 9**: This is called a natural, and no additional cards are drawn by either the Player or the Banker for that round.
- **For the Banker:**
    - **Total of 2 or less**: The Banker draws a third card.
    - **Total of 3**: The Banker draws a third card unless the Player's third card is an 8.
    - **Total of 4**: The Banker draws a third card if the Player's third card is between 2 and 7.

- **Total of 5**: The Banker draws a third card if the Player's third card is between 4 and 7.
- **Total of 6**: The Banker draws a third card if the Player's third card is either 6 or 7.
- **Total of 7**: The Banker always stands.
- **Total of 8 or 9**: This is a natural, and no further cards are drawn by either the Banker or the Player for that round.

Comprehending these rules can enhance your baccarat experience, making it more enjoyable and less financially risky.

House Edge and Commission

Understanding the house edge and the commission on "Banker" bets is essential for baccarat players. These factors significantly influence the game and the player's chances of winning.

- **House Edge:**
    - The house edge on the "Banker" bet is approximately 1.06%.
    - The house edge on the "Player" bet is about 1.24%.
    - The house edge on a "Tie" bet is significantly higher, often around 14.36%.
- **Commission:**
    - A 5% commission is usually taken from winning "Banker" bets.
    - In certain variations, there are no-commission versions with specific rules, such as a reduced payout (e.g., 50% of your wager) for a "Banker" win when the point total is 6. This results in a higher house edge of 1.46% for the "Banker" bet. The house edges for both the "Player" and "Tie" bets remain unchanged.

Basic Betting Strategy

While no strategy can overcome the house edge, understanding common betting strategy can help players manage their bankroll and enjoy the baccarat game more responsibly.

- **Banker Bet Strategy:** Since the "Banker" bet has a slightly lower house edge for 5% commissioned games, consistently betting on the "Banker" is often recommended.

Chapter 3: Betting Systems and Their Flaws

Many gamblers turn to betting systems in the faint hope of overcoming the house edge. This chapter examines popular betting systems and explains why they ultimately fail.

The Labouchere Betting System

The Labouchere system, also known as the cancellation system, involves increasing your stake after every loss with the aim of recovering losses and making a profit. Here's how it works:

- **Setup:**
    - The player writes down a sequence of numbers (e.g., 1-2-3-4-5).
    - The bet size is determined by adding the first and last numbers in the sequence.
- **Gameplay:**
    - If the player wins, the first and last numbers are crossed off the list.
    - If the player loses, the amount wagered is added to the end of the sequence.
    - The process continues until all numbers are crossed off.

Example:

- Sequence: 1-2-3-4-5
    - First bet: 1 + 5 = 6 units
    - If the player wins, the sequence becomes 2-3-4.
    - If the player loses, the sequence becomes 1-2-3-4-5-6.

Despite its logical appeal, the Labouchere system is flawed. If the player encounters a long losing streak, the sequence can become very long, requiring increasingly large bets. This can quickly escalate to bet sizes that exceed the player's bankroll, leading to significant losses.

The table below illustrates a common scenario at real-world casino tables. After 9 wins (41%) and 13 losses (59%), the 23rd bet unit is 24. If this bet wins, the 24th bet unit will be 20. However, factoring in the casino's House Edge, which slightly increases the loss probability, if the 23rd bet loses, the 24th bet unit will be 30. To put these numbers into perspective, if the casino table's minimum limit is $25, then 30 bet units equate to $750. That's $750 of your own money that could be lost to the casino in just a few seconds more!

Bet Number	Sequence	Bet Unit	Result	New Sequence
1	1, 2, 3, 4	5	Lose	1, 2, 3, 4, 5
2	1, 2, 3, 4, 5	6	Win	2, 3, 4
3	2, 3, 4	6	Lose	2, 3, 4, 6
4	2, 3, 4, 6	8	Lose	2, 3, 4, 6, 8
5	2, 3, 4, 6, 8	10	Win	3, 4, 6
6	3, 4, 6	9	Lose	3, 4, 6, 9
7	3, 4, 6, 9	12	Win	4, 6
8	4, 6	10	Win	6
9	6	6	Lose	6, 6
10	6, 6	12	Win	
11	(reset) 1, 2, 3, 4	5	Lose	1, 2, 3, 4, 5
12	1, 2, 3, 4, 5	6	Win	2, 3, 4
13	2, 3, 4	6	Lose	2, 3, 4, 6
14	2, 3, 4, 6	8	Lose	2, 3, 4, 6, 8
15	2, 3, 4, 6, 8	10	Lose	2, 3, 4, 6, 8, 10
16	2, 3, 4, 6, 8, 10	12	Win	3, 4, 6, 8
17	3, 4, 6, 8	11	Lose	3, 4, 6, 8, 11
18	3, 4, 6, 8, 11	14	Win	4, 6, 8
19	4, 6, 8	12	Lose	4, 6, 8, 12
20	4, 6, 8, 12	16	Lose	4, 6, 8, 12, 16
21	4, 6, 8, 12, 16	20	Win	6, 8, 12
22	6, 8, 12	18	Lose	6, 8, 12, 18
23	6, 8, 12, 18	24	?	?, 8, 12, ?, ?

Table 6. Labouchere system betting sequence.

The Martingale Betting System

The Martingale system is one of the most well-known betting strategies. It involves doubling your bet after every loss with the aim of recouping all previous losses with a single win.

How It Works:

- **Initial Bet:** The player starts with an initial bet (e.g., 1 unit).
- **Doubling Bet:** After a loss, the player doubles the previous bet (e.g., 2, 4, 8, 16 units).
- **Win Reset:** After a win, the player returns to the initial bet size.

Example:

- Initial bet: 1 unit
    - If the player loses: Next bet is 2 units.
    - If the player loses again: Next bet is 4 units.
    - If the player loses again: Next bet is 8 units.
    - If the player wins: Next bet returns to 1 unit.

While the Martingale system can work in theory for short winning streaks, it is highly risky. A series of consecutive losses can lead to exponential bet increases, quickly surpassing the player's bankroll and table limits. Additionally, the player risks losing a significant amount of money before achieving a single win.

The Paroli Betting System

The Paroli system, also known as the Reverse Martingale, is a positive progression betting system. It involves doubling your bet after each win with the aim of maximizing profits during winning streaks.

How It Works:

- **Initial Bet:** The player starts with an initial bet (e.g., 1 unit).
- **Doubling Bet:** After a win, the player doubles the previous bet (e.g., 2, 4, 8 units).
- **Loss Reset:** After a loss, the player returns to the initial bet size.

Example:

- Initial bet: 1 unit
    - If the player wins: Next bet is 2 units.
    - If the player wins again: Next bet is 4 units.
    - If the player loses: Next bet returns to 1 unit.

The Paroli system aims to capitalize on winning streaks while minimizing losses during losing streaks. However, it relies heavily on the player encountering frequent winning streaks, which is unlikely in the long run. Just like other systems, it cannot change the fundamental house edge.

The Fibonacci Betting System

The Fibonacci system is based on the famous Fibonacci sequence (1, 1, 2, 3, 5, 8, 13, 21, etc.), where each number is the sum of the two preceding ones. It is a negative progression system, meaning the player increases their bet after a loss.

How It Works:

- **Initial Bet:** The player starts with the first number in the sequence (e.g., 1 unit).
- **Progression:** After a loss, the player moves to the next number in the sequence.
- **Win Reset:** After a win, the player moves two steps back in the sequence.

Example:

- Sequence: 1, 1, 2, 3, 5, 8
    - First bet: 1 unit
    - If the player loses: Next bet is 1 unit (second in sequence).
    - If the player loses again: Next bet is 2 units.
    - If the player wins: Next bet is 1 unit (two steps back in sequence).

While the Fibonacci system is less aggressive than the Martingale, it still suffers from the same fundamental flaw: it cannot change the house edge. Extended losing streaks can still result in significant losses, and the player may quickly reach bet sizes that are unsustainable.

Why Betting Systems Fail

Betting systems are appealing because they promise a structured approach to gambling. However, all these systems share a common flaw: they do not change the house edge. The fundamental mathematics of casino games ensure that the house always has an advantage in the long run.

- **House Edge:** The house edge is built into the game, ensuring the casino's long-term profitability.
- **Randomness:** Each game outcome is independent and random, making it impossible to predict future results based on past outcomes.
- **Bankroll Limitations:** Betting systems often require a large bankroll to sustain long losing streaks, which most players do not have.
- **Table Limits:** Casinos impose table limits to prevent players from making excessively large bets, which can render betting systems ineffective.

By understanding the limitations of betting systems, players can avoid the false hope they offer and approach gambling with a more realistic mindset. The key to responsible gambling is to view it as entertainment, set limits, and never chase losses.

What Does "Never Chase Losses" Mean?

"Never chase losses" is a crucial principle in responsible gambling. It means you should not try to win back money you've lost by continuing to gamble, especially by increasing your bets. Chasing losses often leads to even greater financial losses and emotional distress.

Advantages of Not Chasing Losses

- **Financial Stability:**
    - **Preventing Escalating Losses:** By not chasing losses, you prevent yourself from making increasingly larger bets in a desperate attempt to recover money. This reduces the risk of significant financial harm.
    - **Maintaining Budget Discipline:** Sticking to predetermined limits helps you manage your gambling budget effectively and avoid spending money needed for essential expenses.
- **Emotional Well-being:**
    - **Reducing Stress and Anxiety:** Chasing losses can create a cycle of stress and anxiety as you try to recover what you've lost. Avoiding this behavior helps maintain a healthier emotional state.
    - **Preventing Desperation:** When you chase losses, desperation can cloud your judgment, leading to irrational decisions. Staying calm and composed helps you make more rational choices.
- **Improved Gambling Experience:**
    - **Focusing on Entertainment:** Viewing gambling as a form of entertainment rather than a way to make money helps you enjoy the experience more. You can appreciate the excitement of the game without the pressure of needing to win.
    - **Setting Realistic Expectations:** Understanding that losses are part of the gambling experience allows you to set realistic expectations and enjoy the activity without disappointment.
- **Long-term Sustainability:**
    - **Responsible Gambling Habits:** Developing the habit of not chasing losses promotes responsible gambling practices. This ensures that gambling remains a fun and manageable activity rather than a harmful one.

- **Avoiding Problem Gambling:** Consistently chasing losses can lead to problem gambling and addiction. By addressing this, you reduce the risk of developing a gambling problem.

These practices not only protect your finances but also enhance your overall gambling experience, ensuring it remains a fun and enjoyable activity.

Chapter 4: Money Management Myths

Just as betting systems are flawed, so too are many money management strategies. This chapter debunks common money management myths and emphasizes the importance of responsible gambling.

Setting Win Goals and Loss Limits

While setting win goals and loss limits can help manage the psychological aspects of gambling, they do not change the mathematical reality of the house edge. This section will explore how to set realistic limits and stick to them.

Example:

- **Win Goal:** Decide on a specific profit target for your gambling session. For instance, if you start with $100, you might set a win goal of $50. Once you reach this goal, you stop playing.
- **Loss Limit:** Determine the maximum amount of money you are willing to lose in a session. If your loss limit is $50, you stop playing as soon as you have lost that amount.

While these limits can help control your spending and prevent excessive losses, they do not alter your overall chances of winning. The house edge remains constant, and over time, you are likely to lose more than you win.

The Myth of "Hot" and "Cold" Streaks

Many gamblers believe in the concept of "hot" and "cold" streaks – that a player or a machine can be on a winning or losing streak. This belief can lead to poor decision-making and increased losses.

Reality:

- **Randomness:** Casino games are designed to produce random outcomes. Each spin of the roulette wheel or hand of baccarat is independent of the previous one.
- **Gambler's Fallacy:** Believing that a win is "due" after a series of losses (or vice versa) is a common cognitive bias known as the gambler's fallacy. This belief is incorrect because past outcomes do not influence future results.

Understanding the mutual exclusivity of casino games can help you make more rational decisions and avoid chasing losses based on false beliefs about streaks.

The Falsehood of Money Management Systems

Money management systems, like betting systems, promise a way to control losses and maximize wins. However, they are fundamentally flawed because they cannot alter the house edge.

Common Money Management Systems:

- **Martingale:** Double your bet after each loss to recover previous losses and make a profit.
- **Paroli:** Double your bet after each win to maximize winning streaks.
- **D'Alembert:** Increase your bet by one unit after a loss and decrease it by one unit after a win.

While these systems can provide a structured approach to betting, they do not change the odds of the games. Over time, the house edge will prevail, and the player will likely lose money.

The Importance of Proper Bankroll Management

Proper bankroll management involves setting aside a specific amount of money for gambling and not exceeding that amount. This section will provide practical tips for managing your bankroll effectively.

Tips for Bankroll Management:

- **Set a Budget:** Determine how much money you can afford to lose without affecting your financial stability. This is your gambling bankroll.
- **Divide Your Bankroll:** Split your bankroll into smaller session amounts. For example, if your bankroll is $500, you might divide it into five $100 sessions.
- **Stick to Your Limits:** Never exceed your predetermined session limit, even if you are on a winning streak. This helps prevent significant losses and maintains control over your gambling.

Proper bankroll management helps you gamble responsibly and ensures that gambling remains a controlled and enjoyable activity rather than a financial burden.

Chapter 5: The Illusion of Trends

Casinos often display past play results to create the illusion of trends, suggesting that future outcomes can be predicted based on previous ones. This chapter explains why this is a fallacy and how each game round is independent of the previous ones.

Understanding Independence of Events

Each round of a casino game, whether it's a spin of the roulette wheel or a hand of baccarat, is an independent event. This means that the outcome of one round does not affect the outcome of the next. Here's why:

- **Roulette:** The outcome of each spin is entirely random and independent of previous spins. If the ball lands on red ten times in a row, the probability of landing on red or black on the next spin remains the same.
- **Baccarat:** Each hand is dealt from a shuffled deck or shoe. The outcomes of previous hands do not influence the next hand's results.

Understanding this independence is crucial to avoid falling into the trap of believing that past results can predict future outcomes.

The Gambler's Fallacy

The gambler's fallacy is the mistaken belief that if something happens more frequently than normal during a given period, it will happen less frequently in the future, or vice versa. This belief often leads to poor betting decisions.

Examples of the Gambler's Fallacy:

- **Roulette:** Believing that after several spins landing on black, the next spin is more likely to land on red.
- **Baccarat:** Thinking that if the "Player" hand has won the last five rounds, the "Banker" hand is "due" to win the next round.

The gambler's fallacy ignores the principle of independent events, leading players to make irrational bets based on perceived trends.

The Illusion of Control

Many gamblers believe they can control or influence the outcome of a game through their actions, even in games of pure chance. This illusion of control can lead to increased risk-taking and significant losses.

Examples of the Illusion of Control:

- **Roulette:** Believing that choosing certain numbers or colors based on past results can influence future outcomes.
- **Slot Machines:** Thinking that stopping the reels at a particular moment can affect the result, despite the outcome being determined by a random number generator.

Recognizing the illusion of control can help gamblers make more rational decisions and avoid unnecessary risks.

The Role of Trend Betting

Trend betting involves placing bets based on perceived patterns or trends in past results. While it can be entertaining, it is not a reliable strategy for long-term success.

Why Trend Betting Fails:

- **Randomness:** Casino games are designed to produce random outcomes. Trends and patterns are coincidental and do not provide any predictive value.
- **House Edge:** The house edge remains constant regardless of perceived trends. Trend betting does not alter the mathematical advantage of the casino.

While trend betting can add excitement to the game, it should not be relied upon as a strategy for winning.

Statistical Analysis and Randomness

Understanding the role of randomness and probability can help gamblers avoid falling for the illusion of trends. Statistical analysis shows that random events do not form predictable patterns over time.

Key Points:

- **Probability:** Each outcome has a fixed probability that does not change based on previous outcomes.

- **Random Distribution:** Over a large number of trials, results will tend to align with statistical probabilities, but short-term deviations are common and unpredictable.

Understanding that each game round is an independent event with its own fixed probabilities can help players make more informed and rational betting decisions.

By recognizing the fallacy of perceived trends and the independence of each event, you can make more logical and well-informed choices, resulting in a more enjoyable and responsible gambling experience.

Chapter 6: Effective Strategies for Conscientious Gambling

To gamble responsibly and minimize losses, consider the following strategies. These approaches focus on making informed decisions, managing your bankroll effectively, and maintaining discipline throughout your gambling sessions.

Even Bet

An Even Bet, also known as an even-money bet, is a type of wager in casino games where the potential payout is close to the amount staked. This means that the bet offers nearly a 50% chance of winning, making it one of the less risky betting options available. Because of their relatively high probability of winning, even bets are popular among gamblers who prefer a more conservative approach to betting, aiming to minimize potential losses while still enjoying the thrill of the game.

Examples of Even Bet:

- **Baccarat:** Betting on the "Banker" or "Player" hands.
- **Roulette:** Betting on "Red" or "Black," "Even" or "Odd," and "Low" (1-18) or "High" (19-36).
- **Sic Bo:** Betting on "Small" (total of 4-10) or "Big" (total of 11-17).

Even bet is one of the simplest and most effective strategies to extend your playing time and reduce the likelihood of significant losses.

Flat Betting

Flat betting involves wagering the same amount on each hand or spin, regardless of whether you win or lose. This strategy helps manage your bankroll more effectively and prevents significant losses. However, due to the nature of flat betting and the house edge, you should not expect substantial profits.

How Flat Betting Works:

- **Set a Bet Amount:** Determine a fixed amount to bet on each hand or spin (e.g., $10).
- **Maintain Consistency:** Place the same bet amount regardless of the outcome of the previous hand or spin.

Flat betting is a conservative approach that helps you avoid the pitfalls of more aggressive betting systems.

Set Limits

Setting personal limits for time and money spent gambling is crucial for maintaining control over your gambling activities. These limits help to prevent excessive losses and ensure that gambling remains an enjoyable activity.

Setting Limits:

- **Time Limit:** Decide in advance how much time you will spend gambling in a session (e.g., two hours).
- **Money Limit:** Determine the maximum amount of money you are willing to lose in a session (e.g., $100).

Stick to these limits no matter what. Once you reach either limit, stop playing and walk away.

Avoid Chasing Losses

Chasing losses is the practice of increasing your bets with the goal to recover previous losses. This approach can lead to even larger losses and financial trouble.

Tips to Avoid Chasing Losses:

- **Accept Losses:** Recognize that losing is a part of gambling and accept it without trying to win back lost money.
- **Stay Disciplined:** Maintain your betting strategy and limits even during losing streaks.
- **Take Breaks:** Regular breaks can help you stay focused and avoid emotional decision-making.

By avoiding the temptation to chase losses, you can maintain better control over your gambling activities and prevent significant financial setbacks.

Treat Gambling as Entertainment

Gambling should primarily be seen as a form of entertainment, not a way to make money. This outlook helps maintain a healthy relationship with gambling and alleviates the pressure to win.

Viewing Gambling as Entertainment:

- **Set an Entertainment Budget:** Allocate an amount for gambling just as you would for other leisure activities, ensuring it is money you can afford to lose. For example, set a win goal and a loss limit.
- **Focus on the Fun:** Emphasize the enjoyment of playing the game rather than the outcome. Winning should be considered a pleasant surprise, not the main objective.
- **Avoid Alcohol:** Alcohol can impair your judgment and lead to poor decision-making. Avoid drinking while gambling to maintain clear thinking.
- **Know When to Stop:** If gambling stops being enjoyable or starts causing stress and frustration, it's important to take a break.

By treating gambling as a fun activity and keeping a healthy perspective, you can steer clear of many issues that lead to problem gambling.

Importance of Research and Knowledge

Being well-informed about the games you play can significantly improve your chances of making better decisions. Take the time to learn the rules, strategies, and odds of the games you enjoy.

Research Tips:

- **Understand the Rules:** Ensure you know the rules of the game before you start playing.
- **Learn Strategies:** Study different strategies and understand their strengths and weaknesses.
- **Know the Odds:** Familiarize yourself with the odds and house edge of each game.

Knowledge is power. The more you know about the games you play, the better equipped you will be to make informed decisions.

Maintain a Balanced Lifestyle

Gambling should be just one part of a balanced lifestyle. Ensure that you have other hobbies and interests that provide enjoyment and fulfillment.

Balanced Lifestyle Tips:

- **Engage in Other Activities:** Participate in activities and hobbies that you enjoy outside of gambling.
- **Spend Time with Loved Ones:** Maintain strong relationships with family and friends.
- **Take Care of Your Health:** Ensure that you are taking care of your physical and mental health.

A balanced lifestyle helps to keep gambling in perspective and prevents it from becoming an overwhelming focus.

Recognizing and Addressing Problem Gambling

It's important to recognize the signs of problem gambling and seek help if needed. Problem gambling can have severe financial, emotional, and social consequences.

Signs of Problem Gambling:

- **Preoccupation:** Constantly thinking about gambling or planning your next gambling session.
- **Increasing Bets:** Needing to bet more money to get the same thrill.
- **Chasing Losses:** Trying to win back money lost through gambling.
- **Lying:** Hiding your gambling activities or lying to loved ones about them.
- **Neglecting Responsibilities:** Ignoring work, school, or family obligations due to gambling.

Getting Help:

- **Support Groups:** Organizations like Gamblers Anonymous offer support and resources for individuals struggling with gambling addiction.
- **Professional Help:** Therapists and counselors specializing in addiction can provide personalized treatment plans and support.

Recognizing the signs of problem gambling and seeking help early can prevent serious consequences and help you regain control over your life.

By following these effective strategies for conscientious gambling, you can enjoy the thrill of casino games while minimizing the risks of financial loss. Remember, the key to responsible gambling is to make informed decisions, manage your bankroll effectively, and maintain discipline throughout your gambling activities.

Conclusion

Recap of Key Points

Throughout this guide, we've covered various aspects of casino gambling, emphasizing the importance of responsible gambling and understanding the inherent risks. Let's recap the main concepts:

- **The Reality of Casino Gambling:**
    - The house edge ensures that the casino always has an advantage in the long run. Recognizing this is crucial for making informed decisions.
    - Every game in the casino is designed to favor the house. While short-term winning streaks can occur, the long-term expectation always benefits the casino.
- **The Mechanics of Baccarat:**
    - Baccarat is a popular game with specific rules and variations. Understanding these rules and the house edge associated with different bets is essential for informed play.
- **Betting Systems and Their Flaws:**
    - Betting systems like Martingale, Paroli, Labouchere, and Fibonacci may seem appealing, but they cannot overcome the house edge. Relying on these systems can lead to significant losses.
- **Money Management Myths:**
    - While setting win goals and loss limits can help manage psychological aspects of gambling, they do not change the mathematical reality of the house edge. Proper bankroll management and avoiding the temptation to chase losses are crucial.
- **The Illusion of Trends:**
    - Each game round is an independent event. Believing in trends or patterns is a fallacy that can lead to irrational betting decisions.
- **Effective Strategies for Conscientious Gambling:**
    - Strategies like even bet and flat betting can help minimize losses and maintain control over gambling activities.
    - Recognizing signs of problem gambling, setting time and money limits, and treating gambling as entertainment are essential for maintaining a healthy relationship with gambling.

Final Thoughts

Gambling can be an enjoyable and thrilling activity when approached with the right mindset and strategies. Here are some final thoughts to help you gamble responsibly and conscientiously:

- **Educate Yourself:** Continuously learn about the games you enjoy, including their rules, odds, and house edge. Knowledge is your best defense against irrational decisions.
- **Set Limits:** Establish clear limits for time and money spent on gambling. Stick to these limits to avoid excessive losses and maintain control.
- **Avoid Chasing Losses:** Accept that losses are part of gambling. Chasing losses can lead to larger financial problems and emotional stress.

By following these guidelines and maintaining a balanced approach to gambling, you can enjoy the experience responsibly and avoid the common pitfalls that lead to problem gambling. Remember, the key to responsible gambling is knowledge, discipline, and the ability to walk away when necessary.

Gamble conscientiously, stay informed, and above all, have fun by treating it as a form of entertainment rather than a way to make money.

Appendices

Glossary of Gambling Terms

This glossary provides definitions of common terms used throughout the book to help readers better understand the content.

- **Bankroll:** The total amount of money a player has available for gambling.
- **Commission:** In baccarat, it is the amount collected or deducted by a table's dealer from any winning wager on the "Banker" hand.
- **Hand:** In baccarat, it means the cards that have been dealt to the "Player" or "Banker" in a round of play.
- **House Edge:** The mathematical advantage that the casino has over players, ensuring the casino's long-term profitability.
- **Even Bet:** A bet with nearly a 50% chance of winning, such as "Red" or "Black" in roulette or "Banker" or "Player" in baccarat.
- **Flat Betting:** Betting the same amount on each hand or spin regardless of the outcome.
- **Martingale System:** A betting system where the player doubles their bet after each loss to recover previous losses and make a profit.
- **Paroli System:** A positive progression betting system where the player doubles their bet after each win to maximize winning streaks.
- **Player Pair or Banker Pair:** In baccarat, a "Pair" is formed when the initial two cards of either the "Player" hand or the "Banker" hand have the same point value or are the same face cards (Jack (J), Queen (Q), or King (K)). Two different face cards (e.g., KQ, KJ, QJ) do not constitute a "Pair".
- **Labouchere System:** A betting system where the player writes down a sequence of numbers, with each bet being the sum of the first and last numbers. Wins and losses adjust the sequence.
- **Fibonacci System:** A negative progression betting system based on the Fibonacci sequence, where the player moves to the next number in the sequence after a loss and moves back two steps after a win.
- **Gambler's Fallacy:** The mistaken belief that past events can influence future outcomes in random events.
- **Natural:** In baccarat, a hand total of 8 or 9 with the first two cards, resulting in no further cards being drawn.
- **Tie Bet:** A bet in baccarat that both the Player and Banker hands will have the same total. This bet has a high house edge and is generally not recommended.

Additional Resources

This section provides a list of resources for further reading and support for problem gamblers.

- **Gamblers Anonymous:**
    - A fellowship of men and women who share their experiences, strength, and hope with each other to solve their common problem and help others recover from gambling problems.
    - Website: Gamblers Anonymous
- **National Council on Problem Gambling:**
    - Provides comprehensive resources for individuals and families affected by problem gambling.
    - Website: National Council on Problem Gambling
- **GamCare:**
    - A leading provider of information, advice, and support for anyone affected by problem gambling in the UK.
    - Website: GamCare
- **BeGambleAware:**
    - An independent charity tasked with promoting safer gambling and providing resources to help individuals make informed decisions about gambling.
    - Website: BeGambleAware
- **Therapists and Counselors:**
    - Seek professional help from therapists and counselors who specialize in addiction and problem gambling. Many professionals offer personalized treatment plans and support for recovery.

By utilizing these resources, individuals struggling with gambling issues can find the help and support they need to regain control over their lives and engage in responsible gambling practices.

www.ingramcontent.com/pod-product-compliance
Lightning Source LLC
Chambersburg PA
CBHW072049230526
45479CB00009B/335